STRANGE
~BUT (MOSTLY) TRUE~
STORIES

—— BOOK 5 ——

SADDLEBACK
EDUCATIONAL PUBLISHING

STRANGE
~BUT (MOSTLY) TRUE~
STORIES

www.sdlback.com

© 2020 by Saddleback Educational Publishing

ISBN: 978-1-68021-705-6
eBook: 978-1-64598-074-2

Printed in United States
25 24 23 22 21   2 3 4 5 6

TABLE OF CONTENTS

THE BLOB WAS REAL

The movie *The Blob* came out in 1958. In it, alien goo falls from space. A blob lands on Earth and begins consuming everything in its path. This sounds like science fiction. But the idea actually came from real life.

It was September 26, 1950. Two police officers were on patrol in Philadelphia, Pennsylvania. Their names were Joe Keenan and John Collins. The night seemed pretty normal. Then the men saw something drop from the sky.

The officers wanted to find the object. They drove to where it had landed. What they found was not easily explained. It looked like purple jelly. There were sparkly crystals inside. Mist rose off the six-foot blob.

Collins and Keenan stared at the jelly. They called in for backup. Then Collins decided to touch the blob. His hand came away covered in small bits of goo. These soon evaporated. Scum was left behind on his hand. It did not have a smell.

Backup finally arrived. They were just in time. The blob dissolved right before their eyes. Not a trace was left. Grass under the goo was not even bent. FBI agents were also called. But there was nothing for them to see.

Local media picked up the story the next day. With no evidence, it was not taken seriously. The FBI asked the Air Force for help. But the Air Force said no.

Mysterious purple jelly had fallen from the sky. What was it? Where had it come from?

Nobody can say for sure. But Hollywood loves a good story. This one inspired the movie *The Blob*. A sequel was made in 1972. The original 1958 film was remade 30 years later. In 2017, there were rumors that a third remake was in the works. Even without solid proof, the story of the blob still holds up in theaters.

THE STRANGE TRUTH

- The purple jelly was on Earth for about 25 minutes before it disappeared.

- According to Collins and Keenan, the blob appeared to be alive. They said it seemed to move and shake on its own.

- This was not the first—or the last—report of mysterious space goo. In 1846, people in Loweville, New York, claimed a large pile of smelly, glowing jelly fell from the sky. It evaporated within minutes.

- In 1969, scientists in Australia collected over 200 pounds of goo. The jelly-like substance appeared after a meteor shower in the area. Samples contained amino acids. These are the building blocks of living organisms.

- Phoenixville, Pennsylvania, was featured in parts of the original *The Blob*. Today, the small town holds an annual Blobfest to honor the movie.

JAPAN'S SUNKEN CITY

There are many stories about the island of Atlantis. The first was written over 2,300 years ago. Plato, a Greek thinker, told the tale. In his story, Atlantis was a great empire. But then disaster struck. Earthquakes hit the island. Floods did too. Atlantis sank below the waves. It has been lost ever since.

Stories of underwater cities might seem like legends. But there may be some truth to them.

Japan has a real underwater city. Huge sunken pyramids have been discovered near Yonaguni. This is a small Japanese island. A diver found the stone structures in 1986. At first, many believed they had been made by nature. New findings suggest otherwise.

Fifteen structures have been found in total. Ten are near Yonaguni. Five others were discovered near Okinawa. This is Japan's main island. Parts of a castle have been identified. There are also five temples. Roads connect the structures. Holes in some stones may have once held wooden posts.

There are structures on the nearby coast. These look much like those found underwater. This is one reason people now think it was a man-made city. But more studies are needed to know for sure.

THE STRANGE TRUTH

- Japan's underwater structures are sometimes called the Yonguni Monument.

- Scientists are not sure when the structures were built. They may be up to 10,000 years old.

- One scientist thinks the city sank about 2,000 years ago after an earthquake hit Japan.

- Legends tell of a Pacific civilization called Mu that disappeared underwater long ago. Some think the Yonaguni structures may be what remains of their city.

- Rocks shaped like animals have been found among the structures. Faces have also been found carved into stones.

HEAVY LIFTING

It was 1988. Warren "Tiny" Everal stood in a pineapple field. He was working a job for the Hawaiian Electric Company. A helicopter flew overhead. The pilot was Everal's friend Steve Kux. Kux had been hired to move equipment to the job site. Everything was going as planned. Then suddenly there was a problem.

Kux called to Everal over the radio. His helicopter was having electrical issues. He was going to land. This was not a big deal. The pilot was a pro.

In the past, Kux flew helicopters in the Marines. He was a Vietnam veteran. But he was perhaps best known for his work on *Magnum P.I.* This was a popular TV show in the 1980s. Kux had done all the flying in the show. His famous helicopter had orange and yellow stripes. It was the same one he was currently trying to land.

Kux eased the chopper down. As the helicopter neared the ground, it spun out of control. It crashed into a nearby stream. The pilot was trapped inside.

Everal sprang into action. He was also a Vietnam veteran. Stressful situations were nothing new to him. All he knew was that he needed to save his friend.

The unconscious pilot was in danger of drowning. Another worker ran over to help. He moved Kux so that his head was above the water. Fuel leaked from the chopper. It could blow up at any moment. Everal tried to pull Kux from the wreck. But the pilot's feet were pinned. They were running out of time.

Summoning all of his strength, Everal bent down. With a loud groan, he lifted the helicopter. The other worker grabbed Kux and pulled him to safety. But was the pilot okay? Kux lifted his hand to show he was alive.

Afterward, Everal was hailed a hero. His quick thinking helped Kux survive. But Everal shook off the praise. He later told reporters that he was just happy to have saved his friend.

THE STRANGE TRUTH

* The crash happened on May 6, 1988. Steve Kux was 41 years old at the time.

* Kux's helicopter was a Hughes 500D. It weighed 1,550 pounds. Everal lifted the chopper all by himself.

* Everal noticed that Kux's arm was hurt. He removed his shirt and filled it with ice. Then he wrapped it around Kux's injury.

* Kux was taken to the hospital. At first, he was listed in critical condition. But this was soon changed to fair condition. He had minor injuries, including a broken arm.

* The events of the helicopter crash were caught on film. Today, people can watch the dramatic rescue on YouTube.

TROUBLE UNDER YELLOWSTONE

Yellowstone National Park is full of natural wonders. Millions of people visit each year. Most do not know the park sits on three calderas. These are huge depressions. They are created when volcanoes erupt.

Yes, there is a volcano under Yellowstone. It is still active too. In the past, it has erupted about once every 600,000 years. The last time was 640,000 years ago. Some believe the next eruption is long past due.

But there is more. This is not just any old volcano. It is a supervolcano.

Only about 20 supervolcanoes exist around the world. The last time one erupted was 26,500 years ago. These events affect all life on Earth. Debris blasts high into the sky. This includes ash and dangerous gases. Sunlight is blocked.

Earth's temperature drops. Nothing can grow. People and animals starve.

Will the volcano under Yellowstone erupt? Many are concerned. But scientists say not to worry. They are studying the area closely. The earth gives them clues.

One caldera is 30 miles wide and 45 miles long. A scientist made a discovery in the 1970s. Over 50 years, the caldera's center had risen nearly three feet. It kept rising until 1985. That year, earthquakes shook the park. Scientists guessed that gases were escaping. Then the caldera began to go down.

In 1995, parts of the caldera started rising again. It stopped in 2002. Other areas of swelling were also found nearby.

Fourteen new steam vents opened in March 2003. In July 2004, geysers began erupting at strange times. Ground temperatures soared. Some areas reached 200 degrees Fahrenheit. Parts of the park were closed for a time. They were not safe for visitors.

The current activity in Yellowstone is normal. That is what scientists say. There are 1,500 to 2,500 earthquakes on average each year. But most are too small for people to feel. None have led to a volcanic eruption.

Will we know if a huge eruption is coming? Most scientists think so. They say there will be signs. These can show up weeks, months, or even years in advance. It is also possible that the supervolcano will never erupt again. Scientists are not sure exactly what will happen.

THE STRANGE TRUTH

• A volcano is said to be "super" if at least one of its past eruptions released over 240 cubic miles of material.

• Even if a volcano had a super-eruption in the past, it does not mean it will have one again in the future.

• The Yellowstone supervolcano has had 80 smaller eruptions since its last super-eruption 640,000 years ago.

• When the Yellowstone supervolcano erupted 640,000 years ago, it shot out 8,000 times more lava and ash than Mount St. Helens did in 1980.

• If a supervolcano erupted, it would likely be heard around the world.

THE LOST COLONY

In the late 1580s, over 100 people vanished. They were settlers on Roanoke Island. Over 400 years later, this mystery is still unsolved.

Sir Walter Raleigh was an English explorer. He wanted to build an English colony. It would be the first in North America.

Queen Elizabeth finally agreed in 1584. A colony would be set up on Roanoke Island. This is off the coast of what is now North Carolina.

In 1585, Raleigh sent around 100 men to the island. But this first group faced many problems. They had trouble with the local Native Americans. Their supplies ran low. Within a year, the group returned to England.

Raleigh did not give up. He sent a second group to Roanoke in 1587. This time, whole families made the trip. There were around 115 men, women, and children in all. A man named John White was put in charge.

Later that year, White sailed back to England. The colony needed more supplies. His trip was supposed to be short. But then war broke out between Spain and England. White could not sail back to Roanoke until 1590.

Upon his return, White got a big shock. Everyone had vanished. The colony was deserted.

Two clues were found. "CROATOAN" had been carved on a post. "CRO" was cut into a tree. But what did these words mean?

The island of Croatoan was south of Roanoke. Based on the clues, White hoped he would find the settlers there. Their supplies and knowledge of the area were limited. Perhaps they had joined the Native Americans who lived on Croatoan. This could have helped them survive.

White and his crew planned to go to Croatoan. They would search for the missing settlers. But bad storms rolled in. The ships were forced back to England.

John White never returned to America. He died without learning what happened to the settlers.

———————————————

Several theories have been presented over the last 400 years. Today, many people believe the colony split in two.

The larger group likely traveled to Chesapeake Bay. There, they settled near friendly Native Americans. For a time, the group lived in peace. But then hostile Native Americans attacked and killed them.

A smaller group of settlers likely stayed on Roanoke. They may have later moved to Croatoan.

There are other ideas. The settlers could have tried to return to England. They might have died at sea. Some say they were attacked by the Spanish. Friendly Native Americans may have also taken them in.

Efforts to solve the mystery continue. But

few clues have been found. What happened
to the Roanoke settlers remains unknown.

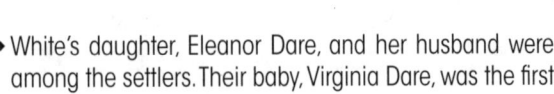

THE STRANGE TRUTH

- White's daughter, Eleanor Dare, and her husband were
  among the settlers. Their baby, Virginia Dare, was the first
  English child born in America.

- White was also an artist. He made many sketches and
  paintings of the land, animals, and Native Americans of
  Roanoke Island.

- Some people think the Roanoke settlers were attacked by
  the Native Americans of Croatoan. This might explain the
  carvings.

- Jamestown, Virginia, became the first permanent English
  colony in America in 1607.

- Today, visitors to Roanoke Island can experience what
  life was like over 400 years ago. They can also watch an
  outdoor play that tells the story of the lost colony.

THE SECRET WINNER

Imagine a lottery jackpot of $1.5 billion. A winner is picked. But they never come forward to claim their prize. This sounds crazy. Winners usually rush to collect their cash. Especially when the prize is huge. It is hard not to get excited about winning money.

This unbelievable situation played out in late October 2018. A Mega Millions ticket was sold at a store in South Carolina. The person who bought it won big. But two months went by. Nobody came forward. The $1.5 billion prize was still up for grabs.

"Everyone's talking about it," the store manager told reporters. "It's a mystery."

Odds of winning were 1 in 302 million. The lucky person had 180 days to come forward. If they failed to do so, the funds would be returned. They would be given back to the states that contributed to the jackpot.

There are rules for using the unclaimed winnings. Each state sets its own. Many put the money into schools. This is what South Carolina does.

South Carolina also allows winners to remain anonymous. This offers protection. Other people might try to steal someone's new fortune. The winner had nothing to worry about. Still, they remained unknown.

Why was this? People had many ideas.

Some thought the winner might have died. Maybe the excitement had killed them. Others guessed the winning ticket had been lost.

Rumors of conspiracy also went around. Was there really a winner at all? Maybe Mega Millions never planned to pay out the $1.5 billion. Perhaps, they just wanted to create a buzz. This would help them sell more tickets.

In early March 2019, the winner finally came forward. This was just a few weeks before the April deadline. The winner chose to keep their name a secret. Why had they taken so long to claim the prize? No reason was given.

This story gets even more incredible. Another customer had wanted to buy a ticket too. The winner let this person ahead of them in line. That means the winner almost did not win.

Lottery officials later put out a statement. In it, they talked about the events leading up to the big win. "A simple act of kindness led to an amazing outcome."

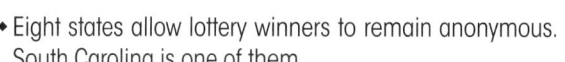

THE STRANGE TRUTH

- Eight states allow lottery winners to remain anonymous. South Carolina is one of them.

- Lottery winners can either take a one-time cash payment or have funds sent to them in smaller chunks over a long period of time. The South Carolina jackpot winner chose a one-time cash payment of $878 million.

- As of 2019, the $1.5 billion Mega Millions jackpot was the second largest lottery prize in U.S. history.

- The owner of the South Carolina store received $50,000 for selling the winning ticket.

- Research shows that Americans let around $2 billion of lottery winnings go unclaimed each year.

A BEE-UTIFUL SEND OFF

Margaret Bell was a beekeeper. She lived in Shropshire, England. In 1994, Bell passed away. Her beloved bees gave her an amazing send off.

Friends and family gathered for Bell's funeral. Afterward, they were treated to an odd sight. Bell's bees had shown up. Thousands buzzed across the street from her house. This was interesting. The bees were kept seven miles away. How did they know where their keeper had lived? She must have made quite an impression on them.

Mourners watched in awe. The bees buzzed on. It was as if they were paying their respects. After an hour, they flew away over the rooftops.

This is not the only story of bees honoring the dead.

Muhammad Ali was a famous boxer. He

died in early June 2016. After his death, many people visited the Muhammad Ali Center. The center is in Louisville, Kentucky. That is where Ali was born.

An estimated 15,000 bees also seemed to honor Ali. They swarmed around a tree outside the center. Making this even more special was a nearby mural. It says: "Float Like a Butterfly, Sting Like a Bee." This is something Ali said before a big match in 1974. The quote sums up the champion's boxing style.

THE STRANGE TRUTH

- Margaret Bell had lived in the same house for 26 years.

- Someone took a photo of the bees at Bell's funeral. It was printed later in a local newspaper.

- A local beekeeper was called in to remove the bees from the Muhammad Ali Center. The bees were rehomed and are now kept by the beekeeper to make honey.

- John Zepka, a beekeeper from Massachusetts, passed away in 1956. Thousands of bees showed up at his funeral.

- Another beekeeper from Shropshire, England, had bees attend his funeral in 1934. The man's name was Sam Rogers.

THE MISSING PRINCESS

In 1918, the Russian revolution was raging. The Bolsheviks captured the Romanovs. They were the Russian royal family. On July 17, they were all killed. But their bodies were not found until 60 years later. Without evidence, no one could prove the entire family was dead.

Rumors flew. Most involved the youngest daughter. She had been 17 years old. Her name was Anastasia.

It was said that some of the Romanovs had sewn jewels into their clothing. This was to keep them safe. When the Bolsheviks shot at them, their bullets hit the jewels. Some believed Anastasia and her brother had survived the firing squad. The family jewels had acted like shields.

Had Anastasia really lived? Several women

came forward. They claimed to be the princess. Anna Anderson is perhaps the best known.

In 1920, a young woman was pulled from a canal in Berlin, Germany. She had been trying to kill herself. The woman was taken to a nearby mental hospital. But she did not have identification. For a while, she refused to speak. Nobody knew what her name was. Nurses simply called her "Miss Unknown."

Another patient had a hunch. She believed Miss Unknown was Russian royalty. Soon others began to think this too. Nobody knew the woman's history. But guesses were made. Some said she was Tatiana. This was one of the Romanov daughters. The woman did not confirm or deny these claims.

Russian exiles began visiting the mental hospital. These people had fled when the Bolsheviks took over. Now they hoped to see the lost princess. She was a link to their past lives. Her supposed survival was a miracle. But was Miss Unknown truly a Romanov princess? Still, she would not say.

Then a man came to see her. His name was Captain Nicholas von Schwabe. He had been a guard for the Dowager Empress. This was the Romanov children's grandmother. After the man left, Miss Unknown spoke up. She told nurses that Von Schwabe had a photo of her grandmother. However, the empress refused to meet with the young woman.

One day, Baroness Sophie Buxhoeveden visited the unknown patient. The baroness had taken care of Princess Tatiana. She said Miss Unknown did look similar. But she was too short. There was no way the young woman could be the princess. Miss Unknown replied that she never said she was Tatiana.

Captain Von Schwabe went to see the young woman a second time. He knew she would not say who she was. Perhaps she might say who she was not. Von Schwabe gave Miss Unknown a list. The names of the four Romanov daughters were on it. She crossed out all but one. It was Anastasia.

Around this time, Miss Unknown started using a new name. Now she called herself Anna Anderson. "Anna" was short for Anastasia. She claimed a guard had found her alive. He carried her to safety. Later, the two fell in love. Then the guard was killed in a fight. That was when the woman had jumped from the bridge.

Anderson's fame grew. Family and servants of the Romanovs came to see her. Some agreed that she looked like Anastasia. Others, however, did not see it. There were people she should have known but did not recognize. She also did not speak Russian.

A Romanov uncle paid for an investigation. It was determined that Anderson was not Anastasia. Instead, she was a Polish factory worker named Franziska Schanzkowska.

But Anderson stood firm. She insisted she was Anastasia. Who could prove her wrong? The bodies of the royal family had not yet been found. Plus, the Russian government was silent on the subject.

By 1968, Anderson had moved to the United States. There she married a rich historian. His name was John Manahan. The couple lived in Virginia. Anderson died in 1984.

In 1991, the bones of the royal family were found at last. By this time, scientists were able to test their DNA. There was no doubt these were the Romanovs. But it seemed that two sets of remains were missing. Had Anastasia and her brother actually escaped?

Scientists compared Anderson's DNA to that of the royal family. There was no match. The DNA proved something else entirely. Anderson actually was Franziska Schanzkowska. Her story had finally unraveled.

THE STRANGE TRUTH

- The Bolsheviks were an extremist political party that came to rule Russia in 1917. They were led by Vladimir Lenin.

- Tsar Nicholas II and his wife, Tsarina Alexandra, had five children. Olga, Tatiana, and Maria were Anastasia's older sisters. Alexei was her younger brother.

- The Bolsheviks shot four of the Romanov's servants. They also killed the family's dog.

- When Anna Anderson married, she changed her name to Anastasia Manahan.

- Plays, musicals, books, films, and TV shows have all been created around the story of Anastasia, the lost Russian princess.

ROBERT THE EVIL DOLL

Robert Eugene Otto was born in Key West, Florida, in 1900. The boy came to be called Gene. He was the youngest of the family's three children.

When Gene was around four years old, he was given a doll. Some say the toy was a gift from the boy's grandfather. It was purchased on a trip to Germany. Others believe the doll was made by one of the family's servants. There are rumors of her cursing it.

In any case, Gene saw nothing wrong with the doll. He named it Robert. That was his own first name. Robert was about three feet tall and made of straw. The boy took the doll everywhere with him.

It soon became clear that Robert was not an ordinary doll. Mr. and Mrs. Otto sometimes heard

Gene talking to Robert. This was not unusual. Children often talk to toys. But someone always answered in a completely different voice. Who was talking? Was it Gene—or was it Robert?

Strange things began to happen in the Otto house. Pictures and lamps fell and broke. Clothing was torn. No matter what happened, Gene always said the same thing. "Robert did it."

Perhaps the boy was right. Some claimed to have heard the doll giggle. Others said they had seen it running up the stairs. Neighbors said they saw the doll move from one window to another. It was all a bit unsettling.

Young Gene was a talented artist. He grew up and went away to school. For several years, Gene lived in Europe. There, he studied and painted. In Paris, he met his wife, Anne.

Then Gene's parents died. Gene inherited their house. When he and Anne moved in, they found Robert in the attic. Once again, Gene became obsessed.

Anne hated the doll. She especially hated her husband's fascination with it. To make Anne happy, Gene eventually put Robert in the tower room.

Gene and Anne died in the 1970s. In 1994, Robert was taken to the Fort East Martello Museum. This is in Key West. The doll is still on display there. Some think Robert is just a harmless toy. But beware. Visitors say their cameras stop working when they try to photograph him. Robert continues to spook people even today.

THE STRANGE TRUTH

- Robert wears a light blue sailor suit. In the museum display, the doll sits in a chair and holds his own toy. It is a small stuffed animal with oversized eyes.

- The doll is over 100 years old.

- One account tells of a night when Gene began screaming. His parents found him in his bed. Furniture had been tossed around his room. Of course, the young boy blamed his doll.

- After Gene's death, Robert remained in the house. A new family eventually moved in. Visitors said they heard giggling and footsteps coming from the attic. Some believed it was the doll.

- Robert has appeared on TV shows, is a stop on a ghost tour, and even has social media pages. A horror movie about the doll came out in 2015.

THE KILLER COUNTESS

Elizabeth Bathory was born in 1560. Her family was rich and powerful. Bathory grew into a beautiful and vain woman. She also became one of history's most terrible murderers.

Some say Bathory was a vampire. She was known to bite her victims. Then she would take a bath in their blood.

At 15, Bathory married Count Ferencz Nádasdy. They moved into a castle together. Bathory had always been cruel. The count might have taught her new ways to torture people. But Nádasdy was often off at war. He may not have known about his wife's cruel practices at all. Most of her crimes took place while he was away.

Nádasdy died in 1604. Around this time, stories of Bathory's brutality began to surface.

The countess worried about growing old. She believed bathing in fresh blood was key. This would preserve her youth and beauty. First, the royal killed her young female servants. Then she went after the daughters of peasants. Promises of work and education brought them to her castle. Young noblewomen were also sent to Bathory to learn good manners. Bathory tortured and killed her victims. Her servants may have helped.

In 1610, people began looking into Bathory's crimes. What they learned shocked them. But Bathory was royalty. She could not be tried. Instead, she was locked in a small room in her castle. The windows and doors were boarded up. Only a small opening remained. It allowed food to be passed to the prisoner. Bathory died four years later in 1614.

THE STRANGE TRUTH

- It is rumored that Bathory viciously murdered over 600 young women.

- Many stories tell of Bathory bathing in her victims blood. Some also tell of her drinking it.

- When authorities investigated Bathory's castle, they found a number of her victims. Some were alive. But they had been horribly tortured. Others were already dead.

- Bathory supposedly stabbed many of her victims. She also stuck them with needles and burned them with hot pieces of metal. Some may have also been starved, beaten, or left in the cold to freeze.

- The rumors of Bathory torturing and murdering young women may have been created so she would lose her money, land, and power.

SAVING LIVES WITH SOCIAL MEDIA

Hurricane Harvey slammed into Texas on August 25, 2017. Harvey was the first major hurricane to hit the U.S. since 2005. Such a powerful storm had not hit southern Texas since 1970.

Harvey dumped over 27 trillion gallons of rain on Texas. This caused massive flooding. Parts of Houston were completely underwater. In the end, there were $125 billion in damages.

Keri Henry lives in Houston. Her home miraculously did not flood. She was very lucky. Flooding forced 39,000 other residents out of their houses.

During the storm, Henry scrolled through Facebook. There were many people asking for help. They could not get in touch with 9-1-1. Henry saw a chance to help. She began writing down the names, addresses, and phone numbers of those in need.

People were stranded. Flood waters continued to rise. Henry knew she had to act fast. She imagined phone batteries running low. Soon these people would have no way to call for help.

Henry decided to call for them. Her list had about 25 people on it. Someone had sent her another list too. This one had the names of people with boats. They were willing and able to help.

Eventually, Henry got through to the fire marshal. The dispatcher thought *she* needed help.

"I am not flooded," Henry said. The woman on the other line was confused.

Henry continued. "I am calling on behalf of 25 families. They could not get through to you."

The dispatcher took all the information Henry had. Then Henry told her about the boaters who wanted to help.

"I'm sorry," the woman said. "But we cannot take any boat volunteer information at this time."

This shocked Henry. People needed to be rescued. Others were willing to help. Why would officials not take their names? Henry took action. She began connecting boaters with victims on her own.

Soon others on Facebook got involved. Posts from people seeking help were shared. Information was exchanged. Rescue teams were organized. Money was raised. Supplies were collected. Henry found it hard to sleep. She wanted to help as many people as she could.

How many people were saved by her efforts? Henry is not sure. But she now sees social media differently. It brings people together when they need it most.

THE STRANGE TRUTH

- To be considered a major hurricane, a storm must be at least a category 3.

- Henry worked alone at first. But soon, a few of her friends stepped in to help. They organized responses and put information into spreadsheets.

- Henry and her friends were able to put together 39 boat teams that had up to four boats each.

- When there was less need for boat rescues, Henry helped organize supplies and donations.

- When Hurricane Maria hit less than a month later, Henry helped get much needed supplies to people in Puerto Rico.

THE MADMAN AND
THE DICTIONARY

Professor James Murray was a busy man. He was putting together the first Oxford English Dictionary. This is also called the OED. It was a huge job that took many years.

In 1879, Murray placed an ad for volunteers. He asked people to send in quotes. These would be used as examples in dictionary definitions.

A man named Dr. William Minor responded to the ad. The doctor's help was priceless. Over 20 years, he sent in thousands of well-written example sentences.

All of Dr. Minor's letters came from Broadmoor. This was a hospital for the criminally insane. Murray guessed that Minor was a doctor there.

In the late 1880s, Murray learned the truth. His friend Justin Winsor visited him. Winsor was the librarian of Harvard College. The men had a good chat. But then Winsor made a comment. What he said shocked Murray.

"Thank you," Winsor began. "For being so kind to poor Dr. Minor."

Murray frowned. "Poor Dr. Minor? What do you mean?"

Dr. Minor, it turned out, was a madman.

———————————————

William Chester Minor graduated from Yale in 1863. This was right in the middle of the Civil War. He joined the Union Army as a surgeon. During the Battle of the Wilderness, a forest fire broke out. Many wounded soldiers burned.

Did the horrors of war drive Dr. Minor mad? It is possible. By 1867, he was showing signs of mental illness. The Army discharged him in 1870. A few years later, he moved to London.

The doctor woke suddenly one night in 1872.

He was convinced there had been an intruder. Later, Minor went out into the street. There, he shot and killed an innocent man.

Dr. Minor was arrested. Then he went to trial. The judge declared him insane. Minor was sent away to Broadmoor.

As a rich man, Dr. Minor had special privileges there. He collected hundreds of books. Many were rare. During the day, Minor seemed fine. Painting and reading were his favorite hobbies. But at night, his mental illness was clear. He claimed people broke into his room. They assaulted him and went through his things. That is what he said. Of course, none of this was true.

In 1880, he answered Murray's ad. Murray and Minor then wrote to each other for years. They finally met at Broadmoor in 1891. The two men talked for hours. To Murray, Dr. Minor appeared quite sane.

In 1910, Minor was released from Broadmoor. He was moved to a similar hospital in the U.S.

Murray died in 1915. Minor passed away

five years later. Sadly, neither lived long enough to see the dictionary published.

THE STRANGE TRUTH

- In 1928, the first edition of the OED was finally completed. It contained definitions for 414,800 words. The huge project had taken 70 years.

- At one point during the Civil War, Dr. Minor had to place a red-hot iron on a man's face. This was to mark him as someone who tried to walk away from his military duties without permission.

- The man Dr. Minor shot and killed was George Merrett.

- Dr. Minor later apologized to Merrett's wife. Over time, the two became friends. Minor sent the widow money to help raise her children. Mrs. Merrett sent the doctor books for his collection.

- Before Dr. Minor helped with the OED, he had worked on Webster's Dictionary of the English Language. Unfortunately, the young doctor made many mistakes and his work was frowned upon.

KING TUT'S CURSE

There is an old story. Anyone who disturbs a pharaoh's tomb will be cursed. Is this true? Some people believe it. Especially after King Tut's tomb was discovered.

Howard Carter was an archeologist. A man named Lord Carnarvon had paid for his expeditions. Both men were from England. Carter had been searching Egypt's Valley of the Kings for years. In November 1922, he was digging near the tomb of King Ramses VI. Suddenly, he found something.

Carter cleared the entrance to the tomb. Carnarvon watched with a hopeful eye.

An opening was made in the doorway. Carter lit a match and looked in. Gold glittered all around.

The tomb contained four rooms. Inside were weapons and chariots. There were statues too.

Other items included clothing and furniture. Ancient Egyptians believed in life after death. Their belongings were buried with them. That way they would have everything they needed in the afterlife.

Carnarvon and Carter realized they had finally found King Tut's tomb. They were very excited. But they soon received a warning. Carter owned a pet canary. When he entered the tomb, his bird was killed. A cobra had slithered into Carter's home and eaten it. Cobras are symbols of Egyptian royalty. Some saw this as a sign. The curse had been released.

Several months later, Carnarvon died. A mosquito had bitten his cheek. The bite became infected. He was dead within three weeks. Cause of death was said to be blood poisoning. Carnarvon's death would not be the last.

A wealthy American man visited the dig site in 1923. His name was George Jay Gould. He quickly became sick. Unable to recover, Gould died of pneumonia within a few months.

Aaron Ember had been present when Tut's tomb was opened. In 1926, he died in a house fire. He could have escaped. But Ember wanted to save the manuscript he had been working on. It was titled "The Egyptian Book of the Dead."

One man had not been at the dig site. His name was Sir Archibald Douglas Reid. Tut's mummy was being sent to a museum. Before that, Reid took X-rays of it. He fell sick the next day. Three days later, he died.

Within 12 years, eight people with ties to King Tut's tomb died. Many felt this was proof of the curse.

Still, nothing awful happened to Carter. He lived to be 64 years old. Perhaps the pharaohs had decided to spare him.

THE STRANGE TRUTH

- Tutankhamen is known as the boy king. He became the ruler of ancient Egypt at age nine. King Tut was only 19 years old when he died.

- The idea of the pharaoh's curse originated in a London stage act in the early 1800s.

- King Tut is rumored to have had a mark on his cheek. Carnarvon's mosquito bite was in the same place.

- It is believed that Tut's tomb was broken into twice before it was discovered in 1922.

A REVOLUTIONARY SPY

There were several great heroes of the American Revolution. George Washington and Paul Revere come to mind. What about Lydia Darragh? Her name is not familiar. But this quiet woman also played an important role during the war.

The Darragh family lived in Philadelphia. In 1777, British troops took over the city. Major John Andre ordered the Darraghs to leave their home. British officers wanted to use it as a meeting place.

Lydia Darragh's family had nowhere else to go. She begged the soldiers to let them stay. Eventually, they agreed. But there was one condition. British officers must be allowed to use the Darragh home whenever they wanted.

On December 2, Major Andre went to

Darragh. He said her house was needed that evening. Her family would have to be in bed by 8:00 p.m. Nobody could leave their rooms. The family did as they were told. But Darragh could not sleep.

Soon her curiosity got the better of her. Darragh got out of bed and tiptoed down the stairs. She hid in a closet next to the parlor. That was where the British were meeting. What Darragh heard was startling. General George Washington and his men were camped at Whitemarsh. This was less than 20 miles north of Philadelphia. The British were planning to attack American troops there.

When the meeting ended, Darragh ran upstairs. She climbed into bed just in time. A moment later, Major Andre knocked on her door. Darragh did not respond. Andre knocked twice more. The third time, Darragh answered. This made it seem like she had been sleeping.

Darragh needed to warn Washington about the attack. That much she knew. The problem was how to do it.

By morning, the woman had formed a plan. Darragh told her family that she needed to buy more flour. She wrote the important information on a small piece of paper. The paper was rolled up and hidden in her needle case. Then the needle case was stuffed deep inside her pocket.

Darragh set off for the flour mill in Frankford. This is a small town north of Philadelphia. First, however, she had to get a permit. This would allow her to cross British lines.

Once at the mill, she left the flour sack to be filled and continued on. Suddenly, Darragh spotted an American officer she knew. His name was Colonel Thomas Craig.

Craig was very surprised to see her. "What are you doing here?" he asked.

The woman knew he could be trusted. Darragh said she had an important message for General Washington. Craig listened carefully. He was stunned. This was exactly the information Washington and his troops needed. They knew the British were planning an attack. But they had no idea when or where it would happen. The colonel promised to deliver the information to General Washington.

But Darragh was nervous. Something might happen to Craig. What if he could not get to

Washington in time? The attack was planned for the next day.

The Rising Sun Tavern was nearby. It was known as a place where colonists shared information. Colonel Elias Boudinot was dining there with some of his men. Darragh decided to give her information to him too.

No one noticed the woman as she entered the tavern. She walked over and spoke briefly to Boudinot. At the same time, she slipped her needle case into his hand. He glanced down at it. When he looked up, Darragh was gone. Boudinot had not even gotten her name.

Boudinot opened the case and searched through it. In the last pocket, he found a small paper. Written on it was the information Washington needed to prepare for the British attack.

Several days went by. Darragh still did not know what had happened. But then British soldiers started to trail back into the city.

About a week later, there was a sharp knock on Darragh's door. It was Major John Andre. He looked mad. Did he know what she had done? Perhaps he had come to arrest her.

"Mrs. Darragh," Andre began. "The night of our last meeting, was your family in bed?"

"Yes," Darragh said. That was not a lie. Everyone else had been in bed.

Major Andre frowned. "Well, I need not ask about you," he went on. "I know you were asleep. It took three knocks before you heard me."

Darragh said nothing.

"One thing is certain," Andre said. "The enemy knew we were coming. They were well-prepared. I can't imagine who could have told General Washington our plans. Unless—"

Darragh barely dared to breathe as she waited for him to finish.

"Unless the walls of this house could speak." Andre looked around angrily. Then he went on. "When we reached Whitemarsh, they were waiting for us. We were forced to march back to Philadelphia like fools."

There were several accounts of how the events unfolded. Darragh's daughter Ann later told the story of her mother's bravery. Some were skeptical. Then in 1909, Colonel Boudinot published his memoirs. The details of his story were slightly different than Ann's. But some facts were the same. One thing was clear. Someone had given Washington information about the forthcoming British attack. Today, many believe it was Lydia Darragh.

THE STRANGE TRUTH

- Darragh's eldest son was an American soldier. One of her younger sons would smuggle coded messages to him about British activities.

- Darragh had a cousin who was a British officer. He helped convince Major Andre to let her family stay in their home.

- The Darraghs were Quakers. Quakers are Christians who are against violence. This was a big reason nobody suspected Darragh of being a spy during the war.

- The Battle of Whitemarsh was the British Army's last attempt at crushing American forces before winter arrived.

- The Americans and the British had several small conflicts at Whitemarsh. But a full-on battle was never launched. British officers called off the attack once they realized Washington's troops were ready to fight back.

BURKE AND HARE

In the 1800s, doctors needed bodies. These were studied and used as teaching tools. But finding a supply of fresh corpses was hard. Few grieving relatives wanted their loved ones' bodies used in this way.

Some doctors found other ways of getting what they needed. Not all were legal. One method was called body snatching. Doctors paid to have recently buried bodies dug up. The fresher the corpse, the more money it fetched.

Where did the corpses come from? Doctors did not ask. Body snatchers never told. There was a good reason. The punishment for body snatching was hanging.

William Burke and William Hare were Irishmen. Both had come to Scotland in search of work. Burke moved into in a boarding house that

Hare helped manage. That was how they met.

Trouble started in the boarding house in December 1827. An elderly man who lived there died. He still owed Hare rent money. But now he could not pay. Burke and Hare had an idea. They decided to sell the man's body to Dr. Robert Knox. Dr. Knox taught at a medical school in Edinburgh.

It was the beginning of a profitable business relationship.

Their next victim was another tenant. This man was very ill. Hare was nervous. A sick person might drive people away from the boarding house. That would put him out of business.

Hare and Burke had another idea. They decided to help the dying man along. Burke smothered the sick man. Then they sold his body to Dr. Knox.

Soon the men had a problem. No more tenants were dead or dying. Burke and Hare took matters into their own hands. They lured a poor woman into the boarding house. Then Burke smothered her. He found this to be a smart method. Smothering a person left no marks on the body.

The murders had begun. Over the next year, Burke and Hare killed 16 people. They sold the bodies to Dr. Knox. He was their only customer.

Over time, the men became reckless. They took too many chances. Other people in the boarding house grew suspicious.

Two tenants were left alone in the house one evening. Curious, they looked around. A fresh body was found under a bed. They reported it to the police right away. Burke and Hare were soon arrested.

Hare turned against Burke. This gave him immunity. It is unclear what happened to him afterward. Many believe he fled from Scotland. Some say·he became a blind beggar in London. Burke was found guilty of murder. He was then hanged. Dr. Knox's reputation was ruined. The medical community slowly pushed him out. Eventually, he moved to London.

This gruesome case had one good result. A new law was passed. This was the Anatomy Act of 1832. It helped doctors obtain more bodies for teaching and studying.

In Scotland, Burke and Hare have not been

forgotten. There is even a children's nursery rhyme about them.

Up the close and down the stair,
In the house with Burke and Hare.
Burke's the butcher, Hare's the thief,
Knox, the boy who buys the beef.

THE STRANGE TRUTH

♦ Before 1832, doctors in the United Kingdom were only legally allowed to use the corpses of criminals who had been sentenced to death.

♦ Part of the body-shortage problem was caused by the Judgement of Death Act 1823. This greatly reduced the number of crimes in the United Kingdom that were punishable by death.

♦ Grave robbing became very common in the early 1800s. Watch towers were built in many cemeteries. Family members would also guard the graves of their recently buried loved ones.

♦ "Burking" is a term that came about after Burke and Hare's killing spree. To "burke" someone is to murder them, perhaps by smothering, without leaving any marks on their body.

♦ After being hanged, Burke's body was dissected by medical students. His skeleton can be found today in the Anatomy Museum at the University of Edinburgh.

ATTACKED IN THE WILD

It was July 23, 2011. Seven teens were hiking in Alaska. They were students at the National Outdoor Leadership School. The group was on day 24 of a 30-day outdoor survival skills course. This final hike was to test what they had learned. With no adults to help, the students had to survive in the wild on their own.

Around 8:00 p.m., the group was walking through a creek. They were moving in a single-file line. The teens had just caught a fish. Their spirits were high. But this soon changed.

Two boys at the front suddenly faced a grizzly bear. They accidently surprised the animal. The bear had a cub nearby. This made the situation much worse. Bears are very protective of their young. With no warning, the bear attacked.

Joshua Berg and Samuel Gottsegen received the worst injuries. They had startled the bear. The two students behind them were also attacked. But their injuries were not as bad.

Those at the rear of the line stayed back. The others had shouted a warning. After the bear ran away, they rushed over to help.

One student took charge. His name was Samuel Boas. He had recently completed emergency medical service training. Boas had probably not expected to use his new skills so soon.

First, the group set off a personal locator beacon. This was for emergency use only. It sent an alert to a nearby rescue center. State troopers were then given the teens' location. Still, it would be hours before help arrived.

While they waited, the students set up a tent. It was very cold. Rain had started to fall. The injured students' wet clothing was removed. Then they were bundled in sleeping bags. They needed to stay warm.

The group had only basic first aid supplies. Boas had to improvise. Dry clothes were removed from backpacks. These were used to make bandages. One boy was having trouble breathing. This suggested he had a lung injury. But Boas knew what to do. He quickly made a bandage from a garbage bag. Then Boas began monitoring the vital signs of his injured friends.

Everyone was very scared. Boas talked to keep them calm. Those who were hurt lost a lot of blood. Luckily, no one lost consciousness.

Six hours later, the teens heard a helicopter. It was about 2:30 a.m. Help had finally arrived.

The four unharmed students were able to leave right away. Berg and Gottsegen could not. Their injuries were too severe. A special medical chopper was needed. Boas refused to leave them.

Two more hours passed. Then finally, the medical helicopter arrived. The three boys were taken to a hospital in Anchorage. Gottesegen and Berg were listed in serious condition. Their injuries were very bad. But they could have been much worse. Boas had helped save their lives.

THE STRANGE TRUTH

- The students in the group were 16, 17, and 18 years old.

- The group was hiking in the Talkeetna Mountains. These are about 100 miles north of Anchorage.

- The teens were not able to run away from the bear. There was no time. They were also unable to use the bear spray they were carrying.

- The students estimate that the bear attack lasted between two and seven minutes.

- Adult instructors were not far from the group. But even if they had been with the students, the bear attack would likely still have happened.

PLANE CRASH IN PERU

It was Christmas Eve 1971. Juliane Koepcke was 17 years old. The day before, she had received her high school diploma. Now she was boarding a plane. Koepcke and her mother were flying from Lima, Peru, to Pucallpa. This is a city about 470 miles northeast of Lima. Her father was working in the Amazon rain forest there.

Their flight started out fine. Then they flew into a horrible storm. Koepcke and her mother held hands. A lightning bolt hit the plane's motor. The plane broke apart.

At first, Koepcke heard the motor and people screaming. Then there was just the rush of wind in her ears. The young woman was still strapped into her seat. But she was no longer inside the plane. Koepcke realized she was free-falling. Then she passed out.

Koepcke fell for 10,000 feet. That is nearly two miles. Amazingly, she survived. She landed somewhere in the rain forest. Her collarbone was broken. There was a big cut on one of her legs. For half a day, the young woman drifted in and out of consciousness.

When she finally woke up, Koepcke began looking for her mother.

"I shouted out," she recalled. "But I only heard the sounds of the jungle."

During her search, Koepcke found a well. She remembered a survival tip. Her father had told it to her once. If she found water while lost, she should follow it downstream. A little stream would flow into a bigger one. Then that would become an even bigger one. Eventually, the water would lead to civilization. The people there could help her.

For 11 days, Koepcke followed the stream. Sometimes she walked through it. Other times she swam. On land there were snakes and poisonous plants. The water was safer. But there were still piranhas and alligators to watch out for.

Along the way, she found other passengers from the plane. They were all dead.

"I was paralyzed by panic," Koepcke said. "It was the first time I had seen a dead body."

She found a bag of candy in the wreck. This was the only thing she ate while walking through the rain forest.

Rescue planes flew overhead. Koepcke could hear them. She tried to get their attention. But the trees were too dense. The planes could not see any wreckage. They definitely could not see one young woman.

By now, Koepcke had been in the rain forest for over a week. Her wounds were becoming worse. Bugs crawled inside them. She was having a hard time standing. But the young woman kept moving.

Finally, she found a hut. It was a good place to stop and rest. The next morning, Koepcke heard people talking. Three Peruvian missionaries stood outside. At first, the men were startled by her. They thought she might be a water spirit.

Koepcke told the missionaries her story in Spanish. The next day, they took her to a nearby hospital. It was there that she was reunited with her father. When she was feeling better, Koepcke guided authorities to the crash site. They were able to find and identify all of the passengers. Of the 91 people who had been on the plane, Koepcke was the only survivor.

THE STRANGE TRUTH

- Koepcke later learned that her mother had survived the crash too. But she had died soon after from her injuries.

- The plane crash led to the largest search in Peru's history.

- It took Koepcke a long time to process the trauma she had experienced in the plane crash. She had horrible nightmares for many years.

- After the crash, Koepcke developed an intense fear of flying.

- In 1998, a documentary called *Wings of Hope* was made about the disaster. For the film, Koepcke returned to the crash site. She even sat in seat 19F, which had been her seat on that fateful day nearly 30 years earlier. The experience, she said, was therapeutic.

THE ELEVATOR GIRL

Betty Lou Oliver was an elevator girl. She worked in the Empire State Building. Oliver would open and close the elevator doors. Then she would work the controls. All day, she moved people up and down inside the skyscraper.

On July 28, 1945, Oliver was operating elevator #6. It was a normal day on the job. Then, just before 10:00 a.m., disaster struck.

A B-25 bomber plane was flying over New York City. This was not unusual. World War II was winding down. Military planes often made routine trips from Massachusetts to New York. But on this day, heavy fog covered the city. The B-25 was flying low and slow.

Suddenly, a skyscraper appeared ahead. The plane quickly turned. But this sent it right into the Empire State Building's 79th floor.

On impact, the fuel tanks exploded. Flames shot down four floors. They also burst out the giant hole in the side of the building. Plane parts flew everywhere. One engine tore through the building. It landed in an apartment across the street. The other engine cut through elevator cables.

Oliver was inside one of the affected elevator cars. She later told the story to her sister.

"The elevator seemed to stop and shudder for a moment. Then it began plummeting downward."

As the elevator fell, it was briefly engulfed in flames. Oliver tried to work the controls. She tried using the car's telephone to call down to the ground floor. But it did not work. The young woman began to scream.

Faster and faster, the elevator zoomed down. Oliver had to hold onto its sides. This was to stop her from floating. In all, the car fell 80 floors. That is about 1,000 feet. How did Oliver survive?

Three things may have helped. First, pressure built up under the falling car. This acted like an air cushion. The cut cables had also piled up in the bottom of the elevator shaft. These absorbed some of the impact.

There was a special elevator part in the sub-basement too. This was supposed to act as a shock absorber. But it did not work as intended. Instead, it slammed through the bottom of the car. Luckily, Oliver was standing off to the side.

Oliver was rushed to the hospital. She was listed in critical condition. Her body was covered in burns. Many of her bones were broken. This included her back. But Oliver would not stay down for long. Just five months after the accident, she returned to the Empire State Building. The brave young woman stepped right back into an elevator and went for a ride.

THE STRANGE TRUTH

- The Empire State Building was the tallest building in the world in 1945.

- All three people on board the airplane died in the crash. Eleven people inside the building were also killed. It was a Saturday, so few people were there working that day.

- Oliver's elevator accident made her a Guinness World Records holder. As of 2019, she continued to hold the record for "the longest fall survived in an elevator."

A REAL-LIFE HORROR STORY

Edgar Allan Poe is a famous writer. He is known for his stories and poems. Some are very scary. One of Poe's most popular works is "The Tell-Tale Heart." But as terrifying as his stories are, they are works of fiction. Readers can sleep well knowing the tales are not real. Except, perhaps, for one.

Poe published *The Narrative of Arthur Gordon Pym of Nantucket* in 1838. In this book, two young boys hide away on a ship. Their journey is not easy. They often face death and see horrifying events unfold.

At one point, the ship becomes damaged. The crew runs low on food and water. Starving, the men are faced with a decision. They can die, or they can eat one of their own.

Straws are drawn. The shortest is picked by

a man named Richard Parker. His fate is sealed. Parker is then killed and eaten. This keeps the rest of the crew alive. Eventually, they are rescued.

This story is made up. But in 1884, Poe's story seemed to come to life. That May, the *Mignonette* set sail. It was traveling from England to Australia. The yacht was old and not made for such a long trip. A strong storm sprang up. When the yacht sank, it was no surprise.

There were four men on the yacht's crew. They managed to escape in a lifeboat. The crew had few supplies. Soon they were hungry and thirsty. One young man decided to drink seawater. But this was a bad idea. It made him very weak.

His crewmates saw an opportunity. They could kill the young man and eat him. This would help them survive. Shortly after their gruesome feast, the crew was rescued.

These events were quite unsettling. It seemed like the crew of the *Mignonette* had lived Poe's story. But that was not all. There was another truly chilling fact. The name of the young man who was eaten by the *Mignonette*'s crew was also Richard Parker.

THE STRANGE TRUTH

- *The Narrative of Arthur Gordon Pym of Nantucket* was Poe's only novel.

- The crew of the *Mignonette* thought they were making the right decision by killing Parker. They doubted he would survive anyway. If he was left to fight for his life, his body would have wasted away. Killing him gave the men a fresh meal.

- When a person eats the flesh of another human being, it is called cannibalism.

- Long ago, cannibalism was considered a "custom of the sea." Sailors who became stranded and had no other means of survival would sometimes resort to eating each other.

- At one point in Poe's story, the crew eats a tortoise that is found among the ship's cargo. The *Mignonette*'s crew caught and ate a sea turtle.